ETERNITY IN OUR HEARTS:

Koudjo's Story

Brenda Ring

Eternity in Our Hearts

Chapter 1

Koudjo's body trembled with cold and fear as he lay in the shallow grave. His hands stung from the lines that had been carved and the powder that had been rubbed into his wounds. He had been told by the witch doctor's minions to lie down in the grave like a dead body, waiting for its master. He could feel something crawling on his face. The scent of the newly dug earth heightened his awareness that recently disturbed creatures had been forced to share his grave.

If Koudjo hadn't been so desperate, he would never have agreed to follow the witch doctor here. After months of misery while many doctors from various hospitals attempted to discover the source of his sickness, no solution was found. He couldn't eat, and he couldn't sleep. His clothes hung loosely on his six foot frame because he had lost so much weight. In Togo, West Africa where he lived, it was part of the culture to consult medicine men who dealt in witchcraft if medical doctors failed to heal. So, when one of his friends suggested that he go to the priest who worshipped the god of death, he decided that he had nothing to lose.

Koudjo had ridden his motorbike six hours to the priest's village, so weak that he wondered if he would be able to make it. Finally reaching his destination, he explained why he had come and waited silently. The priest closed his eyes and murmured words that Koudjo couldn't understand.

“I am seeing someone offering your body to evil spirits to be killed,” the priest’s voice boomed. “You will die soon, unless you offer a sacrifice to my god of death; then you will do a special ceremony in the cemetery at midnight in order to be delivered. Will you agree to do this?”

Without hesitation, Koudjo agreed. Though he was frightened by the uncertainty of what was about to happen, he knew he had come too far to turn back now. At the age of twenty-one, he was too young for his life to be one of misery, ending in a premature death. So, at 11:30 pm, two of the priest’s servants led him through the darkness to the grave they had dug for the ceremony.

There was enough moonlight for Koudjo to see the white paint on the priest’s face and the magic symbols that were painted on his chest and his headband. It had been explained that the priest would walk around the grave seven times. Each time around would represent one day. His mind kicked into endurance mode as he lay terrified and hurting. Each time the priest circled the grave, chanting incantations, it felt as long as a day to him. After the seventh time around was completed, representing the seventh day, Koudjo hauled his weak, trembling body out of the grave. He then had to repeat some words and drink a liquid that made his stomach lurch and threaten to erupt. Once these rituals were over, they returned to the priest's house.

There was another round of ceremonies after they returned. Then, Koudjo was given the assurance that, after seven days, the person who had put the curse on him, or a member of that person's family would die in his place. After the substitution had been made, he would learn of that death and be healed. He paid the priest and started the long journey home to wait for his healing. He took with him more medicine, with instructions to take it at midday. During the difficult journey home he kept thinking that surely, after all he had paid and suffered, his healing was secured.

He finally arrived back in his village around daybreak and barely made it to the rooming house where he lived before collapsing, too exhausted to do anything but wait for sleep to come. But, sleep was not easily found as memories of that shallow grave kept playing around in his head while his whole body throbbed with discomfort.

Chapter 2

He wasn't sure how long he had been asleep, though he knew he had slept sporadically. Looking at the clock, he saw that it was already midday. He still felt exhausted, but knew that his body needed nourishment of some kind. He had no appetite, but was extremely thirsty. He looked to see if he had anything in his apartment to drink and, finding nothing, he made his way into the streets. Amidst the throng of busy shoppers, he bought coffee and a roll from a street vendor and sat on a nearby bench. He was too weak to walk back to his house yet. It was there that one of his friends found him.

“Man, you look like a death mask! Are you all right?” his friend asked with genuine concern.

Koudjo told him briefly about his grueling trip, anxious to return to his room where he could collapse again. He finished his meal as quickly as he could, said good-bye to his friend, and went back to the house. He was prepared to wait out the seven days with as little human contact as possible. Conversation, even with a friend, required more effort than he felt like giving. As a matter of fact, he had no enthusiasm for anything anymore.

Once back in his small parlor, he felt a sense of restlessness and was unable to shut off his mind. He knew that there was no use in going back into his bedroom and trying to sleep. So, he sat in his only comfortable chair and allowed his mind to replay his life up until this point. He desperately wanted to make sense of it all. Why was he suffering in such a way? It had seemed that the whole world was laid out before him just a short time ago. Opportunities were available, waiting for him to reach out and seize the good things that were offered. How could things have reversed so quickly? These questions tormented him as he let his mind wander over details of his life so far.

He was born Koudoga Mawali Nenonene February 16, 1959. His family lived in a small village in Togo, West Africa. In Togo, as well as parts of Benin, Ghana, and Ivory Coast, boys who are born on Mondays are called Koudjo, Kwadjo, Kouadio, or Kodjo. Though his name was officially Koudoga, he was called Koudjo. His father farmed a plot of land outside the village, and his mother purchased quantities of clothes and resold them in the village. They were simple people, nicknaming their first born son as they did simply because he was born on a Monday.

Koudjo and his family attended a village church each Sunday along with many of their neighbors and considered themselves to be Christians. Still, for the rest of the week, they lived much as they wanted, and continued to worship idols as well. When he was twelve years old, his father gave him a small Bible. The Bible was written in Ewe, the local language. Though he never read it, Koudjo carried it with him at all times, almost as though it were a good luck talisman. When he was fourteen, he made the decision to stop attending church.

Koudjo finished school, graduating from college in 1977. He had become fluent in French and English. He wanted to continue his education, studying law, but decided that, due to his financial situation, he needed to seek employment first. Koudjo travelled to Nigeria and was hired by a French company as a Staff Manager because he could speak both French and English. While there, he studied Industrial Radiology for one year and was able to get a job with a petroleum company, working in countries like Senegal, Mali and Congo Brazzaville. After several years of success in this field, He decided that he wanted to try his hand in the business world. He returned home in 1981, excited at the prospect of starting his own business.

Establishing an office at the border of Togo and Ghana, he started a clearing and sales business, supplying goods that were requested by people and delivering the goods to their homes. He had set employees under him to run the business day to day as he directed them and provided oversight. His future looked very promising. Then, without warning, a strange illness took hold of his body.

For weeks, he went from doctor to doctor, hospital to hospital, to no avail. Finally, feeling defeated, he began to seek help from the talisman priests, or "witch doctors." Now, he was in a time of waiting, hoping that he had found the answer to the illness that made his body ache terribly and caused him to be like a skeleton walking.

Just as the time spent in that shallow grave had seemed to go on forever, so did the seven days of waiting to hear about the substitute death. He was so weak that he made the trip to his office only when absolutely necessary, and then only for a few hours. Afterward, he climbed the stairs to his rooms and collapsed again, leaving only long enough to buy necessary food. He saw few people. A rumor had started to circulate among his friends that he had AIDS. Some even said he had cancer. Many of them no longer associated with him, and he had little energy for visiting the few who remained loyal.

The seventh day finally came, lingered, and passed. Koudjo heard nothing, and instead of being healed, his symptoms grew worse. In spite of the disappointment of having gone through all the discomfort and expense without being healed, he still longed for an answer and was unwilling to give up. Then one day when he went to the market, he met one of his few remaining friends. This friend suggested that he needed to visit the witch doctor who worshipped the thunder god. His magic was reportedly amazing. Once again, he set out on a long journey to another remote village.

The witch doctor of the "thunder god" told him that he would have to become a disciple of this god in order to be healed. Desperate, he spent a lot of money and was carried through many incantations. He was given a potion to drink each day while gazing into the sunlight. He was assured that the person who had put a curse on him would be struck by lightning and killed in his place. As he waited for news of the substitute's death, he only became weaker. In addition, his body began to give off a strong odor no matter how often he bathed. Discouragement plagued him, but he doggedly continued to search for healing.

He travelled from his village in Togo across the border into Benin to consult the next witch doctor that he heard about. Once there, he was told that he would have to become the slave of the "snake god" if he wanted to be healed. As part of this ceremony, a sign was carved on his forehead and a powder was rubbed into the wound. He had to drink a potion that was prepared by the priest. As a result, he was assured, the person who had cursed him would be spiritually bitten by a poisonous snake and would die in his place. At that point, his healing would be complete. Again, he waited and hoped for news that such an event had taken place. However, he was disappointed once again.

By then, his body odor was so bad that he was avoided by even some of his most faithful friends. He was ready to give up and prepare to die. As he made a trip for food one day, he saw a friend at the bus stop. Koudjo's misery and despair must have been so pronounced that it stirred compassion in his friend's heart. So, the friend took time to stop and talk with him. After Koudjo had recounted the attempts he had already made to find healing, another suggestion was given.

"Have you tried the health god?" the friend asked. "Many have found relief through him."

So, once again, Koudjo made a long journey to seek the help of yet another witch doctor. There, he was given a long list of items that he was to purchase and bring to the priest so that medicine could be made for his healing. He paid the witch doctor a great deal of money and wearily went from shop to shop purchasing the required items. As he started the grueling journey home, a strong inner voice began to speak to him.

"You have looked to all these gods for healing. You have worshipped these idols, have drunk these potions, have worshipped these other gods, but you haven't once looked to your Creator. How can you stand before your Creator when you die after having done all these abominable things?"

Koudjo tried to ignore the inner voice. For the next four days he was unable to sleep. By now, all his friends had abandoned him. His body stank, he was a walking skeleton, and rumors were circulating that he had HIV. He felt sure that he was dying. Then, the inner voice came for the second time. It was so intense that he could no longer ignore what he knew to be true.

In a moment of strong resolve, he rose up, took the idols, talismans, and medicines and went far from his house to the bush to bury them. He then returned to his rooms and fell to his knees holding the Bible his father had given him when he was twelve years old.

"My Creator," he cried out, "Forgive me for forgetting about You and turning to these other gods! Now as I am dying, I want to make peace with You before I come to meet You. I don't want to face Your judgment!"

Not knowing what else to do, he took the Bible and began to rub it all over his body, as though it might have some healing power of its own. He began to ask for healing, with the thought running through his mind that the Scriptures had the power to heal him. This whole experience lasted for about thirty minutes. He became dizzy and fell on his bed and into a deep sleep. It was about 3:00 pm, and Koudjo, after not sleeping for four nights, slept until 10:00 am the next day. He woke up hungry for the first time in days.

He went to a nearby restaurant and ordered a lot of food. As he shoveled the food into his mouth, the thought came to him that he was eating like a camel. For the first time in many days, he smiled. He felt lightness in his heart, the evidence that his hope had been restored. When he had eaten all he could manage, he went back home and fell back into bed for another eight hours of sleep.

Chapter 3

When Koudjo awoke, he was immediately aware that his body no longer had the deep aching that had marked his days for so long. As he began to move around, he realized that nothing hurt. After bathing and getting dressed he also became aware that the horrible body odor was gone. He didn't feel sick at all! For the first time in months, he felt completely well, as though he had never been sick. He couldn't believe that such a miracle had happened. He began to jump and dance in his room, shouting loudly enough for the whole house to hear.

"God has healed me!" he shouted, running from room to room in the house, surprising all the other tenants. As he continued to sing about Jesus' healing him and to dance with delight up and down the halls, his neighbors came out to watch in amazement.

Not stopping for anything, Koudjo danced on outside, jumped onto his motorbike, and rode to the homes of all the friends who had turned their backs on him. He was eager to share the good news with each of them. He forgave them for their abandonment and wanted only to share about Jesus and what He was able to do. He wanted them to know that all the gods they had referred him to were powerless, and that Jesus was the only One who could save! They were the first people he preached to, telling them that man's gods were useless. Immediately upon hearing, two of those friends burned their idols in front of Koudjo and went to buy a Bible. That day marked the dynamic beginning of Koudjo's ministry and service to his newly found Lord.

He knew nothing about theology, nothing about doctrine, only that Jesus had given him new life! Driven by that knowledge alone, he travelled about 148 miles from Lome, Togo's capital city, to his parents' village. There, he shared the Good News with his mother. She was so touched by the story her son had told that she immediately threw away her fetishes and put her faith in Jesus. Koudjo also went from house to house in the village proclaiming the healing power of Jesus. His excitement was so great that he just couldn't contain it. Later, many others in his family and the village where he had grown up also became believers.

Koudjo pondered all that had happened: his trips to the witch doctors, all that they had told him, their failure to bring healing, and his encounter with the Living God. He began to read his Bible, thirsty for more of the Lord who had saved him. One day he came across a verse in Ecclesiastes that made him shake his head in agreement.

"He has made everything beautiful in its time. Also, He has put eternity in their hearts." Ecclesiastes 3:11

He realized then that the witch doctors had a deep sense of the principle of substitution. Someone needed to suffer the punishment in the place of man in order for him to be delivered from death. With this truth burning in his heart, Koudjo returned to each of the witch doctors to tell them that their magic didn't work, but that Jesus had willingly died in order to be that substitute. He stated clearly that only Jesus could bring life and healing. Their response was unwillingness to forsake their gods and the good income their type of medicine provided. So he left knowing that he had done all he could to bring them to the truth.

……………………………………………………………………………………

……………………………………………………………………………………

At first, Koudjo did not join a church. When he wasn't working in his business, he spent his time studying the old Bible his father had given him and sharing the Gospel. The Bible became a precious tool for him, and he finally appreciated the gift given by his father so many years before. He wasn't worried about going to church, only about knowing Jesus. Because he didn't join a church, people in the area began to mock him, calling him a preacher without a church. Finally, he realized that he also needed to be part of a local church family and to receive training in order to serve God more effectively.

As he continued to go from house to house and preach about Jesus, he also felt the conviction that the call of God was upon his life. Then one night he had a dream. In the dream, a man appeared and said to him, "But you."

The phrase was repeated several times. Then he was told to read 2 Timothy 4:1-5:

"In the presence of God and of Christ Jesus, who will judge the living and the dead, and in view of his appearing and his kingdom, I give you charge: Preach the word; be prepared in season and out of season; correct, rebuke, and encourage with great patience and careful instruction. For, the time will come when people will not put up with sound doctrine. Instead to suit their own desires, they will gather around them a great number of teachers to say what their itching ears want to hear. They will turn their ears away from the truth and turn aside to myths. ***But you,*** *keep your head in all situations, endure hardship,* ***do the work of an evangelist,*** *discharge all the duties of your ministry." (NIV)*

His instructions were clear, leaving no room for doubt. He made the decision from that moment to lay down the rest of his life in service to the Lord who had saved him from sin and death. Then, he faced the challenge of finding a church that would help him prepare for the call on his life.

It was a big challenge. He knew that some of the churches were not in the truth. Some of them had pastors who even used magic powers as part of their church's ministry. Others used the Gospel only as a tool to extract money from the poor and needy. He was afraid that his lack of experience might land him in an unsound church such as one of these. Finally, in 1983, he joined with a strong charismatic church.

Though this was a Bible based church and Koudjo learned a great deal from being a part of that ministry, there was a doctrinal issue that became insurmountable. When he sought to go to the Bible school that was connected with the church, he learned that only those who could speak in tongues were given scholarships. He told the pastor that he was willing to pay for his own tuition, but he was still denied entry. Koudjo began to seek the gift of speaking in tongues. He fasted and prayed to that end without receiving what he prayed for.

There was a night when the pastor gathered with those seeking to speak in tongues as evidence of having received the Holy Spirit. As the Senior Pastor laid his hands on each individual, he instructed them to begin to say whatever sounds came to mind. Some of the people present began to speak in tongues, but others didn't. Koudjo was one of the ones who didn't. He was so disappointed that he began accusing God.

"God, what have I done for you to refuse to give me the gift of tongues? Precious Jesus, did I commit any sin? Why this injustice? "

He was so disappointed that he fled from the church that night, even forgetting his motorbike and walking home. It was a terrible moment in his Christian life. At that point, he stopped going to that church and set out to find a genuine Bible college. He continued to share the Gospel everywhere he could. He also decided to read the Bible through on his own, from Genesis to Revelation.

While reading 2 Corinthians 3:17 one day, the verse leapt off the page for him. It said : *"Now the Lord is that Spirit: and where the Spirit of the Lord is, there is liberty."* These words went deep into Koudjo's heart, bringing the healing light of the Holy Spirit to the moment of darkness that had wounded him. He had thought that the inability to speak in tongues meant that he didn't have the Holy Spirit. Without the Holy Spirit, how could he even be saved? How could he have the power needed to proclaim the Gospel?

Now, God was making it clear that Jesus is that Spirit. It became clear that since Jesus dwelt in his heart by His Spirit, no other experience was necessary for him to be saved. He understood that it wasn't a matter of receiving something new, but a matter of yielding to that same spirit that raised Christ from the dead. Though he still didn't know why some were given the gift of tongues while others were not, he felt free from this dangerous bondage. Peace and hope flooded his heart once again.

Finally, in 1992, he found a Bible institute with sound doctrines called IBL (Institut Biblique de Lome). There was a very good team of teachers who was able to give solid, Biblical training to the students. He graduated from IBL in 1996. He stayed on as a teacher at IBL until the year 2000. Koudjo didn't know when he started teaching at his old school that one day the woman who would become his wife would also attend there.

Chapter 4

In his second year of teaching at the Bible Institute, Koudjo went to visit his friend, Antoine, who had started a church in the nearby village of Kagome. Antoine had invited Koudjo to come and visit and consider helping in the church. He met with Antoine and other pastors to discuss church planting and other aspects of the church's ministry. They were also making preparations for a celebration the next day that would involve a number of other pastors. Koudjo excused himself from the meeting to take a bathroom break. On the way back, he passed a kitchen area where he saw a young woman working by herself.

"Hello," he greeted her. "Are you working here all alone?"

"Hello. Yes, I decided to stay and make sure everything is ready for the meal tomorrow," she answered.

As they continued to chat, Koudjo learned that her name was Pierrette and that she lived quite a distance from the church. Further conversation revealed that she had walked the distance and planned to walk home as well. It was getting late, and it was a very dark night. The thought of all the dangers that might be lurking caused him to be concerned for her safety.

"Would you allow me to walk with you when you are ready to leave," Koudjo asked with concern. "It would ease my mind to know that you arrive home safely."

"Thank you. That would be very nice, if you are sure it's not too much trouble," Pierrette replied with a smile.

So, that evening marked the beginning of his relationship with his future wife. As they walked together, he learned that she had a small son. She had lost her husband when her son, Roland, was only ten months old. She had recently moved here to help Antoine and some others with starting this new church.

When the pastors had finished their meeting, Koudjo went to the kitchen and found that Pierrette had finished her work. As they walked out into the pleasant night air, they fell comfortably into conversation about the Lord and their work in the ministry. Though it was a long distance, the time seemed to pass quickly. When they reached the house where Pierrette lived with several other families, they said good night, knowing that before long it would be time to go back to the church for the next day's meeting.

After Koudjo had left Pierrette at her home, he had the long walk back to think about this interesting lady. She was obviously a very hard worker. Working late to prepare all that food at the church without help, and supporting herself and her child, was proof of that. Also, their conversation had shown him that she was very intelligent and dedicated to serving the Lord. The realization came to him that, if he were seriously looking for a wife, she would be the kind of woman that would interest him. The thought that lingered, though, was that she had one of the most beautiful smiles he had ever seen.

Koudjo made no plans to see Pierrette again at that time, though he did see her occasionally when he attended Antoine's church. He did, however, begin to pray for the Lord to show him clearly whether or not he should pursue the relationship. He knew that he was called to be a pastor and that he would need to marry someone of the Lord's choosing. Koudjo knew also that his own choice would be for someone with a gift of hospitality, someone who was hard working, and a prayer warrior. He felt that Pierrette seemed to meet all of *his* qualifications. Not only that, but she was very beautiful. So, he prayed.

....

....

Pierrette was the second born in a family with ten children. Her father was a hard working carpenter who was a real dictator in his home. No one in his family dared to cross him. Like his father and grandfather before him, he was also an idol worshipper with many idols. Twice a year he would offer sacrifices to the main idol in the middle of his house. He was not a very agreeable man, and more than anything, he hated any mention of the Gospel of Jesus Christ.

Pierrette went back home to live with her parents for a short while after her husband died. Eventually, she was able to get a place to live in a large house with many other families. There, she cared for her son, supporting them by cooking and selling rice and fish outside the apartment house. She also took in sewing for people to supplement her income.

Koudjo's friend, Antoine, had been pastor of a church in Pierrette's village at that time. Through Antoine's ministry, her younger brother, Boris, became a follower of Jesus. His father immediately disowned him when he found out about his son's conversion. This did not discourage Boris from sharing about his newly found Savior with Pierrette. Boris's heart went out to his sister, knowing the pain she had endured at the tragic loss of her husband and the struggle she had in raising her son. He went to her house to share the Good News of Jesus, believing that He would meet her needs, both spiritual and physical. Pierrette immediately rejected his attempts to share the Gospel with her. She clung to the beliefs of her father and was unwilling to turn from them and risk his disapproval.

Boris returned to her house later, bringing Antoine with him. Antoine shared the plan of salvation with her also. He returned more than once in an attempt to convince her that she needed to accept the gift being offered to her. Again, she refused. As he left that day, Antoine offered one last comment.

"Nobody knows when his last day of life will be on this earth. It is urgent for you to make a decision to accept Christ before that day."

Soon after Antoine's visit, Pierrette was involved in a motorbike accident and was seriously injured. As she lay in the hospital, not knowing what the outcome of her injuries would be, she was almost paralyzed with fear. What would happen to her young son if she died? Then Antoine's words came back to her. Worse still, what if she died and was separated from Almighty God forever? It was at that moment that she prayed, asking Jesus to forgive her for her sins and to come into her life. That day marked the first real peace and comfort she had experienced since she had lost her husband.

She attended church with Boris as soon as possible after leaving the hospital. She also went to their father to share the Gospel with him. He became so enraged that he nearly slapped her. She left quickly, before he could unleash his anger on her. It grieved Pierrette to realize that she was no longer welcome in her father's house. It grieved her even more to think of his spiritual state. She made it her mission from that time on to pray for the Lord to soften her father's heart.

Pierrette and Boris remained steadfast in their newly found freedom in Christ, even in the face of their father's judgment. They both became active members of Antoine's church, serving God and helping to spread the Gospel in their village.

After some years, Antoine decided to go to Kagome to start his church there. Pierrette and Boris went with him to be a part of that new church planting. It seemed only natural for Antoine to enlist the help of his old friend Koudjo from the Bible Institute. Two years later, Pierrette and Boris were also enrolled in the same Bible Institute where Koudjo and Antoine had met.

That night of their first meeting when Koudjo had walked her home, Pierrette had enjoyed the conversation and the concern for her safety. After Koudjo had said good night and left, Pierette had leaned against the closed door for a moment, unaware of the faint smile that lit her face. She was touched by the gentleness of this tall, strong man whose physical presence had certainly made her feel much safer on the long walk home. She didn't really worry about being alone at night as much now that she knew the presence of Jesus in her life. Still, the comfort of someone showing concern for her and the physical presence of such a one felt good after the months of sorrow and loneliness. The Lord had done a great deal of healing of that hurt, but she had determined to not marry again. So, she didn't feel ready for the feelings that were stirring in her heart. Not willing to examine them too closely, she pushed them aside, committing them to the

Lord for safe keeping. Her job now was to care for her son and to serve the Lord in doing whatever He directed. With that resolve, she went to check on her sleeping child.

Chapter 5

Koudjo prayed for a year, all the while going about his teaching duties and continuing to help in Antoine's church. He had seen Pierrette periodically at the church, but had not pursued the relationship. He was able, though, to observe more of her servant's heart at work and her dedication to a ministry of prayer. Finally, he felt the assurance that he should share with Antoine (her pastor and his friend) his feelings and his interest in her. He knew that timing was crucial, and that Antoine, knowing much about Pierrette's life, would be able to give him sound advice. Somehow, Antoine didn't seem at all surprised to hear of Koudjo's interest in Pierrette.

Antoine agreed that it was the time for Koudjo to begin to see more of Pierrette and to share his feelings with her. Thus began their courtship, tentatively at first, then growing to the point where Koudjo felt it was time to ask her to marry him. Her answer should not have surprised him now that he knew more about her dedication to prayer. She wanted time to pray specifically about the Lord's will for her life; so he waited.

In the year 2000, Koudjo was transferred to a church in a town called Tsevie where he would serve as Assistant Pastor. Then, two years later, in 2002, he became Senior Pastor of that church. It was that same year when Pierrette also received the assurance that this marriage was the Lord's will for them. So, on August 3, 2002, they were married. Their marriage formed a bond in the spirit realm that would become a powerful instrument for the furtherance of the Kingdom of God.

Not only had Koudjo gained a wonderful wife, but he had also gained a precious son. From the beginning, he considered young Roland as his first son. He and Pierrette joyfully began their life and ministry together, secure in each other's love and in knowing their Lord had brought them together.

In 2005, their second son, Benaya, was born. They were thrilled to have another son. They named him after one of David's men who had been mighty in battle. Koudjo's prayer was that his second son would be mighty in serving the Lord just as Benaya had been in serving in David's army.

It was also in 2005 that Koudjo's pastor asked him to go to Benin to start a new work there. Koudjo knew that such a move must only happen if it was the Lord's will for them. They had a new baby and such a move would not be easy on the family. His response was that he would pray about it. One night after he had started praying, and after he had mentioned the possibility of a move to Pierrette, Koudjo had a dream.

In the dream, a man came to him and said, "Wake up and read John 15:16."

He was very groggy and was tempted to turn over and go back to sleep, planning to read the verse in the morning. Again, the man spoke, "Koudjo, wake up now and read John 15:16. If you wait, you will forget."

He sat up in the bed so abruptly that Pierrette woke up and asked him what on earth was wrong. He patted her shoulder reassuringly and said, "Pierrette, please get the Bible and read John 15:16 to me."

As Pierrette read the verse, Koudjo sensed the Holy Spirit giving him strong direction.

"You did not choose Me, but I have chosen you and appointed you that you should go and bear fruit, and that your fruit should remain, that whatever you ask the Father in My name He may give you." (NKJ)

There was no doubt in Koudjo's mind then about what the Lord's will was for them. Taking the Bible from her, he closed it. The difficulty of the move meant nothing now.

"Pierrette, God has spoken. We are going to Benin." He told her gently. There would be no more sleep that night as Koudjo began to think about the move and the powerful way the Lord had shown him the next step in their journey.

So, when Benaya was six months old, they relocated to Benin. With this move, their lives would take a lot of twists and turns. As Koudjo did the ministry tasks he had been called to do, Pierrette focused on making a comfortable home for them and caring for the children. In addition, she did what she could to bring in income to help support them. She travelled outside the village to bring honey from the bee keepers to sell. She also sold pens and other such items in the village. But, most importantly, she prayed. Her habit was to get up at 4:00 a.m. and pray for two hours before the children needed her attention. Then, she prayed throughout the day as she felt led by the Holy Spirit.

Whenever things became difficult, as they sometimes did, they would remind each other of that night and the verse from John that the Lord had given Koudjo in the dream. Koudjo was thankful for a wife who worked so hard for the family and who covered him and their ministry in prayer. He knew that the Lord had chosen for him well.

Pierrette had never dreamed when she lost Roland's father that she could ever marry again, but she knew that the Lord loved her so much that He had brought Koudjo into her life. No longer was she alone, even though Koudjo travelled much of the time. When he returned home, the joyful sound of his booming laughter ringing in their home blessed her heart. His love of music and his deep voice raised in song enriched their lives and were a delight to her. Her God was so good!

Chapter 6

In 2007, Koudjo founded "Mission La Bible Parle" or, in English, "The Bible Speaks Mission." The focus of this newly founded association was to make disciples of Jesus Christ who would, in turn, make disciples in remote villages. As a beginning, Koudjo chose thirteen young men that he had led to Jesus. He had made the decision to make himself available to be their mentor and life coach. For a full year, they met four times a week to study scriptures. His goal was to invest in them sound teachings and the principles of Christianity. As they grew and matured in Christ, they started village ministries, house cell groups, and a bus ministry. The goal was for them to also make disciples, thus carrying the message of Jesus further into remote areas.

The year of 2009 was one of great blessing. For one thing, their first daughter, Laura, was added to their family. Koudjo and Pierrette were delighted with her birth and the new dimension that she added to their family. As loving as Koudjo had been with his sons, Pierrette noticed an even greater tenderness when he held his tiny daughter. And, as much as she loved her sons, it was so special to finally have a daughter.

Also in that year the mother church with which Koudjo was affiliated planted a daughter church in the village of Adjaigbonou. In addition, one of Koudjo's pastor friends introduced him to a man named Dr. David Nelms, the President/Founder of TTI (The Timothy Initiative). Dr. David had come for the first time to West Africa to share the church planting vision of his organization. As Koudjo listened to him, he realized that this vision was very similar to his own. As they became further acquainted, Dr. David asked if Koudjo would be willing to join with TTI as their West Africa Director. Koudjo believed that it was the Lord's will for him to accept Dr. David's offer. A whole new ministry endeavor was the result of that decision.

After joining with TTI, Koudjo led the training of twenty pastors, ten from Benin, six from Ghana, and four from Togo. They quickly set to work in their part of West Africa, training others to plant churches and to disciple still others to do the same.

Once the new converts were taught the basics of Christianity, they were given five days to share the Gospel with five people. Then they were supposed to take the new believers they had led to the Lord and teach the basics of Christianity to them. They used the book,

Disciples Making Disciples, a publication of TTI. It was from this model that the new house churches were formed. More intensive studies were made available for those who felt called to continue on in the ministry and who wanted to become more prepared for their calling.

During 2010 and part of 2011, 381 church planters were trained. Of the 381 who were trained, 277 "graduated" from the program. This meant that those 277 planted a new church and trained more people to go out and do the same. All together, 321 new churches were planted by 2011, most of them being house churches. This resulted in more than 6,000 new disciples who began to follow Jesus.

Early in 2011, Koudjo received word from the daughter church in Adjaigbonu of extreme need in that area. There had been a severe famine and disease had ripped through the village, leaving many dead. Of the dead, many of these were children. Koudjo contacted some of their Canadian pastors who sent funds for help. They bought food, blankets and medicine and went to the village to distribute them.

While he was in the village, an old woman approached Koudjo and began to plead with him to take her granddaughter with him when he was ready to leave. The young girl, named Liza, was very thin, half naked, and covered with sores. The grandmother explained that the child's parents had deserted them and moved to another village. They were illiterate and didn't even know for sure how old Liza was. Koudjo guessed that she was around nine years old. The grandmother explained that Liza's young brother had already died, and she couldn't bear to watch Liza die as well.

Koudjo was overcome with compassion as he looked into the grief stricken eyes of the grandmother, then at the suffering child. He felt that to deny this request would surely end in the child's death. He called Pierrette on his cell phone and explained the situation.

"Pierrette, if I leave her, she will surely die. I want to bring her home to live with us."

Pierette's immediate response was that, yes, of course he should bring her home. After contacting the child's parents and receiving their permission to take Liza, he took her back home with him. So, they now had two sons and two daughters. Koudjo watched as Pierette lovingly nursed Liza back to good health. It was a joy to see her become stronger as she was fed nutritious food. Watching her shy personality unfold in the secure environment of their family made Koudjo very happy.

Chapter 7

In July of 2011, the Democratic Republic of Congo (DRC) was also ready to open training centers. Thirty pastors from Rwanda, Burundi, and DRC were ready to be trained so they could begin. Koudjo was asked to go and lead in training them. The training dates were from July 11-21, 2011. He decided to fly from his home base in Cotonou to Goma on July 7 in order to arrive in time to meet with Athanese, the coordinator, the next day.

"Pierrette, this is a very important journey." he shared as he was preparing to leave. "Please pray for our success as I go." He hugged her and the children, assuring them of his love and that he would be home soon.

At 12:00 pm, local time, the Boeing 727 of Hewa Bora took off. The length of that flight was to be about five hours, with the connecting flight taking another four hours before reaching the final destination. Just before landing, Koudjo was settled in row 4C, just behind the curtain of the Business Class, at least as settled as one over six feet tall is able to get on an airplane. He was looking out the window at the poor weather conditions. All was quiet as Koudjo and the other passengers anticipated the imminent landing, eager to deplane and stretch their legs after the long flight.

In the next instant, utter chaos set in. Koudjo heard a loud blast. Then the plane went down, landing in a forest next to the runway where they were intended to land. Koudjo felt his body being thrust on to his right side, with something that felt like iron blocking him from moving. He tried with all his might to move his body, to no avail. It was then that he realized why he couldn't move. He was buried in the dead weight of lifeless bodies. He lay there, confused, fighting panic. After what seemed an eternity, he could hear people shouting and the sound of fire truck sirens. Then came blasts that sounded like bombs.

"Lord," Koudjo prayed fervently, "If you aren't going to take my life during this crash, please, Lord Jesus, please, ***do not*** let me be burned! Save me from the fire while everything is blasting everywhere!"

To his amazement, he suddenly felt as though the Lord was right next to him. He had never experienced His presence in such a way before. Then he heard the strong inner voice:

"Koudjo, you can see that nobody in this plane can help you, no one is capable. Only someone who is outside this plane can come and rescue you. It is the same with man's sin. Likewise, Jesus is come from above, outside of man's sin nature, to save the sinner."

"Yes, it is clear, Lord." Koudjo replied with a new depth of understanding.

Psalm 30 immediately came into his mind.

> *"I will exalt you, O LORD, for you lifted me out of the depths and did not let my enemies gloat over me. O LORD my God, I called to you for help and you healed me. O LORD, you brought me up from the grave; you spared me from going down into the pit. Sing to the LORD you saints of his; praise his holy name" (NKJ)*

At that point, a spirit of praise and thanksgiving washed over him.

"Thank you, Heavenly Father, in the name of Jesus!" Koudjo prayed. "Thank you that You didn't let my enemies rejoice over my death! Thank You for not allowing Pierrette to become a widow after just nine years of marriage! Thank You for not allowing my children to become orphans! Thank You for loving me!"

Then, Koudjo began to shout with all his strength: "Someone is alive down here, HELP ME! There's someone alive, COME ON!"

The most welcome sound he'd ever heard came a few moments later, when a voice said: "Take the dead bodies off him quickly! The fire is coming!"

When they'd removed the last dead body, a Congolese soldier said words that Koudj would never forget.

"Hey, you man, God loves you because He hid you down there. Look at all the bodies we pulled from the top of you."

Koudjo told him he was 100% correct. God's great love had saved him! Then, the last blast came from the cockpit, throwing black smoke into the air. As the smoke billowed around them, they ran with all their might. Koudjo caught a glimpse over his shoulder of the plane as it was enveloped in flames.

The two soldiers practically dragged Koudjo along as they narrowly escaped the flames. They took him to Kisangani University Hospital for first aid. It was very dark and overcast from the storm, but he could see that the ground was littered with injured survivors, some of them badly burned. There was wailing and tears everywhere as people searched for their loved ones. He heard someone say that there were at least seventy passengers who were dead. Another forty were badly injured, some with third degree burns. As he was being moved to a place for treatment, he saw a baby, about ten months old, who seemed to have escaped any injury. Tears came to his eyes as he thanked the Lord for protecting this little one.

As people were searching for loved ones, a man shone his flashlight on Koudjo's face, hoping to find his uncle who had been on board the plane. When he realized this wasn't his uncle, he started to move on, but Koudjo called him back.

"Please, I know no one here in Kisangani," Koudjo pleaded. "I am on my way to train a group of pastors in Goma. Please let me use your phone to call my contact in Goma so they'll know I survived the crash."

The man handed him his cell phone, and Koudjo placed the call. He was greatly relieved when Athanase came on the line.

"This is Koudjo." Then he began to proclaim: "I am alive, and Satan is a liar! It's God's plan for me to come to

Goma to hold the training, and I will come, by all means. NOBODY can stop me! I am on my way!"

Apparently Athanese had already heard about the crash because Koudjo could hear him shouting, "Alleluia! Alleluia! Alleluia! Our facilitator survives!"

Andre, the owner of the cell phone, could hear Athanase's shouts of praise in answer to Koudjo's proclamation. His heart was so touched that, from that moment, he became the contact point between Koudjo, Athanase, the TTI office in the United States, Pierrette, and Koudjo's friends. Koudjo had no doubt that God had placed Andre there at that point in time for His purposes.

The only injuries that were found in Koudjo's body at that time were bruised ribs and other bruises from having been at the bottom of the heap of bodies. For reasons known only to God, Koudjo and a ten month old baby were the only ones who survived the crash with no serious injury.

………………………………………………………………………………………

………………………………………………………………………………………

As usual, Pierrette had gotten up to pray the morning of the plane crash at 4:00 am. Then, at around 6:00 am, she got the broom and began to sweep the front of the house as she always did. Suddenly, she heard an audible voice say:

"Drop the broom, enter your room, and give thanks to the Lord."

She turned around to see who was talking, to find no one. The voice was so clear and powerful, though, that she left the broom and went into her room to thank the Lord as directed. She wondered why, after having already prayed for two hours, the Lord would give such an order, but she was quick to obey.

It wasn't until Koudjo called at 6:00 pm (DRC local time), hours later, telling her he had just survived a plane crash that she understood. God had prompted her to thank Him ahead of time for the miracle He was about to perform. Pierrette gave thanks again from the bottom of her heart. What a wonderful God! He had not only spared her husband from death, He had allowed her to be a part of the miracle through prayer. It was such a comfort to know that He had been in full control all along.

Koudjo enjoying training others

Koudjo with top TTI leaders Fredgy, Jared, and Andre.

Chapter 8

Using Andre's phone, Koudjo made a number of other calls that night. He called Jared Nelms, who was David Nelms's son and the International Director of TTI, and was encouraged by him. Jared assured Koudjo that TTI would do everything possible to help. Then, he called another friend, Pastor Real, pastor of a ministry he was affiliated with in Canada, and was met with utter disbelief.

"Nobody could survive a plane crash and only a few hours later be talking as clearly as you are!"

The next day, as Pastor Real read news reports from the internet, he learned that his friend had indeed survived by a miracle of God. That miracle was to become a tool that the Lord would use to reach many people in days to come.

Koudjo's new friend, Andre, left the hospital for a while. Then, he returned later that night with his sister, Eugenie. He informed Koudjo that they were members of the Assemblies of God. They wanted to move him to a private clinic to be thoroughly checked out. So, he was moved to the Stanley Clinic. He was examined and given something to help him sleep. The following morning, July 9, 2011, he woke up and went to the bathroom to take a shower. When the hot water cascaded over his body, a spirit of praise rose up in him, and he began to sing a French song in a booming voice.

> "He saved me, He saved me
> Blessed be His name
> My Savior
> Be blessed for eternity!"

He was so overcome with joy that he wept loudly as he sang. He didn't realize that he could be heard all over the clinic. It was as though the clinic seized to function for a few minutes as they all listened to Koudjo's joyful weeping and singing before the Lord. He couldn't help giving praise and thanksgiving to Almighty God. When he came out, he saw the nurses lined up, so touched that they, too, were crying. There was no doubt in their minds as they listened to Koudjo praising his Lord that he was a walking miracle. There was also no room for doubt as to the source of that miracle.

....

....

When Koudjo had told Athanase the day before that Satan is a liar, and that he would surely come and conduct the seminar, he was proclaiming by faith. He had no idea how it would happen. He had lost everything he had with him on the plane: his laptop, his camera, his money, his bags, etc. But, he had escaped with his life, and none of the rest mattered. He knew that the Lord would work out the details.

That afternoon, a man dressed in a suit, followed by some other men, came into his room. The man explained that the President of Democratic Republic of Congo would be coming to express his compassion for the families who had lost someone in the crash. He went on to say that he thought the President would probably take survivors like Koudjo back to Kinshasa in his private plane.

"I am not going back to Kinshasa," Koudjo tried to explain. "I am on a mission to Goma."

The man kept insisting until Koudjo finally got fed up.

"I am not going back to Kinshasa," Koudjo stated firmly. "Though I appreciate your concern about my health and comfort, it is the President of all presidents, whose name is Jesus, Who is sending me on to Goma."

As the man walked away with his companions, Koudjo knew that he must be thinking that Koudjo had to be the most foolish man he had ever seen not to accept such an offer. Nevertheless, he knew that it was not foolishness, but the wisdom of God that caused him to decline.

Only a few minutes after the men had departed, Andre came to the clinic to announce that his uncle, for whom they'd been searching, had been found dead. His uncle's children were sending a small jet to bring his body home to Goma. Andre told him that he felt sure that Koudjo would be allowed to fly back with them. They drove to the mortuary where the uncle's body was stored.

The coffin with the uncle's body was being transported by car to the airport, and Koudjo and Andre followed in another car. Once there, Andre negotiated a seat on the jet for him. A few minutes later, they were airborne, headed for the completion of the assignment God had given.

During the flight, the children of Andre's uncle cried and mourned their father for the entire time. Koudjo's heart went out to them. Then, he began to think about the grace of God. Questions began to reel in his mind.

"Yesterday, this man was alive on the plane, just like me. Why am I not the one in the coffin? Am I better than he is? "

Then the answer settled over him, bringing peace. No, it was just by grace, not because he was more spiritual, more valuable, more experienced, or better in any way. He understood then that the Sovereign God is in full control, that if He has a plan for your life, no one can take your life until God allows it to happen. God just wasn't through with him yet.

When they landed in Goma, and Koudjo left the plane, he saw the many people who had gathered to welcome the body of Andre's uncle home. When he saw the many celebrities and expensive cars that were there, he realized how truly important this man had been. As important as he had been, his time on earth had ended.

Chapter 9

Athanase, who was at the airport to welcome Koudjo, took him straight to a good clinic in Goma to be thoroughly checked out. They discovered that, in fact, one of his ribs was broken. Otherwise, he was fine. They kept him for observation until July 13, when he was released. Koudjo asked Athanase to take him directly to the Baptist church where the men had gathered for training.

Koudjo began the meeting by praising God for His mercies and love. Then he shared his testimony of the crash, joyfully proclaiming that no amount of persecution or troubles on the road of life can stop the movement of Jesus all over the world.

"What I learned from the plane crash," he shared with those at the training, "is that if God, your Creator, has not finished His plan for you in this world, there isn't anybody or anything that can stop your life. No event can overrule God's plan in your life."

On July 19, 2011, the training ended, and Koudjo and Athanase travelled to Kigali/Rwanda. That same day, Koudjo was invited to appear on a Christian Radio program to give his testimony and be interviewed. So many people were touched by the story of his miraculous escape from injury and death that numerous calls began to pour in from listeners, praising Jesus.

After returning home, he was invited by a Christian organization to come to a meeting that was being held in a local hotel and to give his testimony. When he finished, a man came up to him.

"I know this is a Christian Association," the man began, "but I have come to the hotel for business. I have never cared about Jesus before today. Your story has caused me to determine to go to my home right away to burn all my magic books. Now, I will follow Jesus."

As he turned to leave, he asked Koudjo to remember him in his prayers. It was at that moment that Koudjo really understood Romans 8:28:

"And we know that all things work together for good to them that love God, to them who are called according to his purpose." (KJV)

God had taken a terrifying, tragic event in Koudjo's life and was using it to bring about good in the lives of many people. He knew that he loved God and that he had been called by God for a purpose that was much greater than his own.

This verse was again brought to his mind in 2012, when he was invited to Quebec, Canada to attend a convention in Mont-Joli. Koudjo's ministry, Mission La Bible Parle was affiliated with Assemblee Chretienne La Bible Parle, which was based in Canada. For that reason, he accepted the invitation. As he shared his testimony there, many more were blessed by all that God had done. It served to boost the faith of many people who attended. So it was that God took something that Satan had intended for evil and turned it to good.

Chapter 10

When Koudjo returned home after the plane crash, it was hard for Pierrette to resist clinging to her husband a little. She had come so close to losing him, but God had been merciful. She knew that Koudjo would need to travel again soon. His work of spreading the Gospel was so important to both of them, and there was so much to be done! Yet, even though she trusted God to continue His care for them, her human emotions sometimes wanted to take over. As they sat together in the evenings listening to music or talking after the children were asleep, she savored his physical presence and held on a little tighter than usual. She was just thankful for any time out of the busy schedule that they had together.

Pierrette found her life to be rich and blessed, even with Koudjo's frequent travel. In addition to caring for the four children, she had a ministry in their village of visiting hospitals and talking and praying with patients. She also led a ministry to elderly women, particularly widows. That, along with time spent in intercession, kept her very busy. She marveled at how God had shown His mercy over and over again in her life. Still, her heart longed to see her father, Daniel Gbehossou, come to know her Savior. So, she continued to pray.

The decision was made in 2014 to locate the TTI office in Togo. Pierrette and the children moved to Togo and helped Koudjo's brother Elie Mawunyo, also a pastor in their ministry, to start a TTI house church. When Koudjo was not travelling, he joined them in the house church. Once Koudjo was there with them, Pierrette expressed again her concern for her father.

"I wish there was some way we could reach my father with the truth of the Gospel, Koudjo," she said one evening as they were talking together. "Now that we are living back in Togo, I have been praying for a way."

"Maybe there is a way for you to re-connect with him," Koudjo responded thoughtfully. "Maybe we could invite him to our home just for fellowship. We don't have to preach to him, just love him."

They decided that they had nothing to lose. When they asked him to visit, he finally agreed. After several visits, they invited him to a church service with the house church. They stressed that nobody would pressure him, they just wanted him to be able to enjoy the fellowship. He agreed to come if they would pick him up since he lived a good distance away. After he had attended two services, they asked if he wanted to continue. To their delight, he said yes.

One day during the church service, Daniel, her father, raised his hand and said he wanted to give a testimony. A hush fell over the group as they waited anxiously, uncertain of what would come next.

"I fought the Creator for a long time," he began. "I thought I was strong. I discovered that my Creator is almighty. I surrendered my life to Jesus, and since then, I am free. I am now ready to meet Him in peace any time from now."

There were tears and much rejoicing as Pierrette witnessed the answer to her many prayers. The hard, unkind man she had known her father to be had been transformed into a tender-hearted man of God. Always, she had trusted God to answer her prayers, but she was totally amazed at the goodness of the Lord now that it had happened.

At his own initiative, he personally threw every idol out of his house, one by one. His brothers and sisters were dismayed when they learned what had happened. Still, he continued to follow the Lord, going against generations of idol worshippers in his family.

A short time later, Pierrette's father became ill and could no longer talk or walk. His brothers and sisters began to persecute Pierrette. They accused her of bringing a curse on her father. They believed she was the cause of his denying the god of their ancestors, bringing the anger of the spirits and causing his sickness. It was a time of great testing for both Pierrette and her father. Yet, Pierrette continued to give thanks that her father's soul was secure and to pray for his healing.

Chapter 11

The year of 2014 was filled with more travel for Koudjo as he continued to work with TTI to spread the Gospel and to train more leaders. He attended a leadership retreat in Bengalura, India in June. Then, in July more than sixty pastors gathered in Liberia to attack the challenge of making disciples in more remote areas. In addition, he travelled to some of the new churches to encourage and assist in whatever ways he could.

As he travelled, he heard stories of the impact that the TTI training centers were having in different areas. One story in particular impressed upon Koudjo the power that the correct teaching of the scriptures has to transform lives. A young preacher who had been preaching the "Prosperity Gospel" was invited by a friend to attend the

TTI training center in his area. This young preacher had used the scriptures previously to intimidate his congregation and to coerce them into giving more and more money to the church. He would invite preachers of the "Prosperity Gospel" from Nigeria to preach at his church also. He was able to provide for himself financially very well while his flock suffered.

At first, he attended the training to please his friend and because he was curious. As time went on and he spent more time studying the scriptures in the training, he began to realize what a horrible thing he had been doing in his church.

"I was shocked at how I had been wounding the flock of Jesus," he admitted. "I began to weep loudly. The Holy Spirit pointed out my error to me and convinced me that I needed to change. I wasn't feeling condemnation, but experienced deep regret for my past and the desire to change."

He said that he had received the power to make that change from the Holy Spirit. He cancelled the preachers from Nigeria who were scheduled to come to his church in the future. He then preached with a new joy the true Gospel, with Jesus being the focus of his messages. Though his congregation was already noticing the change in him, he publicly repented for the way he had preached a false gospel and had taken advantage of his church.

"Now, instead of manipulating my brothers, I am ready to wash their feet and serve them. I would prefer being hungry to seeing them in need. I would rather be thirsty than to see them without enough water," he stated, going on to thank God for His great compassion.

Stories like these were very encouraging as Koudjo continued to travel and keep the strenuous schedule that the ministry demanded. Concerns for the safety of church planters and new believers weighed on his heart as Christians in many parts of Africa were being persecuted. Stories of the transformation of lives in the midst of the danger were especially helpful.

Then, in September of 2014, Koudjo was asked to come for the first time to the United States to meet with David and Jared Nelms at the TTI headquarters in West Palm Beach, Florida. He was to bring a report of the progress being made through TTI in West Africa and to share in a number of churches.

Soon after he arrived in the United States, Dr. Greg Kappas, the Vice President of TTI, drove him around the beautiful city of West Palm Beach. As they toured the city, Koudjo appreciated its beauty and order. Remembering his trips to Canada, he realized that in both countries, there was a beauty in the architecture and an orderly transportation system. He knew that many of the leaders in Africa had been educated in the United States and Canada. One question nagged at him even after returning to Africa. Why weren't they able to bring the knowledge from the United States that they had gained back to Africa and reproduce the same order and architectural beauty in his own country? That question continued to puzzle him.

Koudjo met with Dr. David, Jared and Greg at the TTI offices and later attended an evening event, "Night for the Nations." This event featured Andre Harriott from Kenya, Fregy Mathew from India, and Koudjo. These men, along with Dr. David and Jared, told of what God was doing around the world through TTI. There were many stories shared of those whose lives were changed by the power of Jesus Christ because of the work of TTI. It was a golden moment for Koudjo as he joined in the celebration of what the Lord had done.

Koudjo then participated in various missionary conferences and shared in churches in Florida, Tennessee, Virginia, and Alabama. The high point of the trip, a moment he knew he'd never forget was when he was at Liberty University in Lynchburg, Virginia. After attending a prayer meeting, they had gathered for a time of refreshment. In walked a dear friend of his, Cortland. Cortland had traveled for hours from Maryland to see Koudjo and attend the meeting. He was carrying with him a gift of four books. One of these was Living by Revealed Truth: The Life and Pastoral Theology of Charles Haddon Spurgeon. It was a gift that he would treasure, along with the friend who had given it.

Koudjo was impressed by how hard the Americans worked to make life easier for people and at the abundance that he saw all around him. Still, he was surprised at how much complaining he heard among the American people. He was also amazed at how much the American people ate. It had to be due to such abundance, he reasoned. His country suffered from more famine and poverty, resulting in a more difficult life for his people.

He couldn't help thinking that if Americans could compare their situation with that of people elsewhere, they would have a greater appreciation for the grace of God. It would help them to realize that what they have is not due to their great strength and intelligence, but due to His grace. Still, Koudjo was thankful for those in America who were willing to share their abundance to help others who were in need around the world.

As he returned home to a humbler sort of life than many Americans live, he felt extremely blessed to be back in his own country with his family. After the plane crash,

Pierrette was always a little apprehensive when he traveled. He tried to contact her immediately when he arrived at a destination in order to spare her any anxiety. She was always greatly relieved when she heard from him, and especially when he had returned home safely again. When he returned home their times of being reunited as a family were precious.

Chapter 12

Not long after Koudjo had returned home from the trip to the United States, something heartbreaking occurred. When they moved to Togo, Koudjo had contacted Liza's birth parents as a courtesy to let them know that his family was relocating. Her parents were in agreement with having Liza moved to a different city. So, it was a total surprise when they contacted Koudjo later saying that they wanted to take Liza back to live with them again.

Koudjo and Pierrette were in shock at the news. They considered Liza to be their daughter and had treated her as such, sending her to school along with their own children and loving her as their own. She had blossomed into a secure, delightful girl. They could only imagine how difficult such a change would be for her. As they agonized over this turn of events, they realized that legally they had no recourse. Though it broke their hearts, they had to let Liza's parents come and take her back.

This was especially hard for Pierrette who had spent so much time with Liza, lovingly helping her adjust to life with them. Now, she had to let her go into an uncertain future with only prayers and good memories to accompany her. Pierrette determined to pray fervently for her little Liza. They also determined that if they were ever to rescue another child, they would do so only if they could make the child legally theirs.

This happened in October after Koudjo had returned home from the United States. Though that month brought much pain, in His great mercy, the Lord comforted their hearts with another miracle that off-set the pain of losing Liza.

One Sunday, since Pierrette's father was no longer able to come to the church services, Koudjo decided to bring the church service to him. They carried him out to the main room to sit with them as they worshipped the Lord and prayed to Jesus, the Healer, on his behalf. Though he could not talk to them, Pierrette could see in his eyes that he was blessed by God's Presence as they worshipped and prayed.

A week later, he was completely healed, and able to walk and talk again. He was able to attend church again. After years of idol worship, Daniel had been saved, and healed. In December, they all gathered together for a family celebration and to thank God for Daniel Gbehossou's life. A family portrait was taken, with both natural and spiritual family included. It was a day for great rejoicing.

After eighteen years of prayer, Pierrette's father came to know Jesus. Then, the God of Mercy answered their prayers for his healing. It renewed her hope and confidence as she now prayed for the Lord to protect and comfort their Liza.

Koudjo was grateful to Almighty God for bringing comfort and assurance to his dear wife in this way. At the age of 83, Daniel was now looking forward to being baptized. His father-in-law's salvation and healing were the best gifts of all during the year 2014.

Chapter 13

Koudjo began the year of 2015 by concentrating on the development and raising up of more leaders as the work with TTI continued to grow. He traveled periodically to encourage young churches and to meet with leaders throughout West Africa in an effort to strengthen the ministry. Prayers were concentrated on targeting unreached and Muslim regions in Africa.

He also began to work on a financial plan for his family and ministry with strategies that would carry them through until the year 2020. The world's economy was uncertain, but he trusted the Lord to guide him as he planned for the future. As he endeavored to be a good steward, he knew the Lord would carry them through any difficult times ahead by His grace.

He and Pierrette prayed together for God's guidance in every small detail concerning their family life. They realized how quickly their young family was growing up. Roland was now in medical school, and the younger two were also moving along in school. They prayed for integrity as they parented these precious ones and managed the ministry tasks they had been given. Koudjo and Pierrette knew that their actions were being observed by their children, along with their attitudes. It mattered how they set their priorities. As they prayed together, the Lord began to show them what their focus should be in the New Year.

"Pierrette," Koudjo began one evening when they had spent time in prayer. "I think the Lord is saying that it is not so much what we do for the Kingdom which counts the most. I think the main issue is obedience. Obedience to what Jesus is saying is worth more than our performance or achievement."

Pierrette smiled and nodded in agreement.

"Yes, we have already had many difficulties along the way," she added. "We'd be foolish to think that we won't have even more as time goes on. We'd be more foolish still to choose anything other than obedience."

Koudjo opened his Bible and began to read from Psalm 115:

"Oh Lord, who may abide in Your tent? Who may dwell on your holy hill?

He who walks with integrity, and works righteousness, And speaks truth in his heart.

He does not slander with his tongue, Nor does evil to his neighbor, Nor takes up a

Reproach against his friend; - - - He who does these things will never be shaken."

As Koudjo closed his Bible, they both knew that the Lord had spoken clearly to them, giving them the sense of direction for which they had been praying in this New Year.

Once again, Koudjo thought of Ecclesiastes 3:11

"He has set eternity in their hearts."

Solomon, the writer of Ecclesiastes, had tried everything the world had to offer in an attempt to find the things that would satisfy. He followed every false pathway trying to find what he later concluded could only be found through a relationship with God. In His mercy, God had set eternity in the hearts of man, that sense of longing to have a relationship with his Creator. Yes, setting obedience as a top priority in order to maintain that life-giving relationship was the Word that God had spoken to them. They both knew that Word would carry them through another year.

Chapter 14

In July of 2015, Koudjo attended a retreat in Lome, Togo with pastors and missionaries from "The Bible Speaks, Africa." It was a rich and refreshing time for the servants of God as they prayed for each other, for other leaders, and for integrity in the handling of the finances of the ministry. They ended the powerful prayer time by washing each other's feet, just as Jesus had done to show His love and caring for His disciples. The time together was so rewarding that they decided to meet twice a year. As evil in the world seemed to be intensifying, the need to encourage and pray for one another seemed to be growing greater.

After being home for only a few days, Koudjo was preparing to leave on yet another trip. This journey brought a great sense of excitement to his spirit. He was meeting other TTI leaders and pastors in Egypt. It was a land that was full of history, cited more than 700 times in the Bible, a country that had never changed its name. It was the country where Moses had lived and a country that had given refuge to Jesus and his family. Now, God seemed to be indicating that He wanted them to move into that area as part of the Great Commission:

"Therefore go and make disciples of all nations, ---" Matthew 28:19 NIV.

As he talked with the children the night before he left about where he was going next, Laura asked him a question.

"Papa, is it the same Egypt as the one in the Bible, the Egypt that's in the sky?"

Koudjo gave a little chuckle and said that yes, it was the same Egypt as in the Bible, but it wasn't in the sky. It was here on Earth. It reminded him of his own belief when he was a young boy that the Garden of Eden was in the sky. It was questions such as these from his sweet child that he treasured. He felt the Lord must also delight in His children when they ask for answers to things too big for them to understand without help.

Sometimes, the enormous task set before him caused Koudjo to go running to his Father God to ask questions which probably also brought a chuckle. Without that recourse, life on this Earth would be more than he could bear at times. Still, he could see signs of the Father's hand at work all around him.

On his way to Cairo the next day, he reviewed the latest statistics on the churches that had already been planted in West Africa. He knew that through the work of The Timothy Initiative, 3,344 new churches had been planted. Yet, there was so much left to do.

Then, the Holy Spirit gently reminded him that his obedience was all that was required of him. So, he opened his laptop and went to his Facebook page. He shared about the meeting in Egypt, giving background information and even sharing the anecdote about Laura's question. Then he asked those prayer warriors who were his "friends" to pray for an awakening in Egypt. He asked them to pray for a special visitation from God in that beautiful country.

Having been obedient, he closed his laptop and leaning back, closed his eyes. With a smile on his face, he fell into a deep and restful sleep for the rest of his flight. Whatever happened next was in God's hands.

Chapter 15

In December of 2015 Koudjo was again in the United States, this time for a leader's retreat for some of the top leaders in The Timothy Initiative. The retreat was being held at the Veldhuizen Cheese farm in Dallas, Texas. While at the retreat, Dr. Nelms shared that he had been contacted by a wealthy man who wanted to do something to bless those dedicated men of God who were gathering there. Knowing of the many sacrifices made by these men, especially time spent away from their wives and families, this man wanted to send them on an "all expenses paid" tour of Israel. Even more significant was the decision to include the wives in the trip as well.

At first, Koudjo just chuckled to himself, believing this to be a joke. Then, he realized that it was no joke. God was indeed blessing them through this wealthy man. Such news was almost too great for his mind to comprehend. He had never dreamed of being able to visit Israel. He smiled, hugging this news to himself, deciding to wait until he returned home to share it with Pierrette. Such a thing was too special to share through a phone call.

Koudjo continued on to New Mexico and Indiana before returning home in order to visit churches that partnered with The Timothy Initiative. Each moment that he wasn't actively engaged in meetings and speaking, his mind would return to the secret that he was holding on to. Then a smile would come to his lips. Always, as he neared the end of such a journey, he would begin to think of Pierrette and the children and the things he missed about home. He would start to get hungry for his favorite foods of smoked fish stew and pounded yams that Pierrette always prepared for his first meal back. With this news to share, he was even more eager than usual to return home.

On December 15th, Koudjo returned home to find Pierrette at the airport to meet him as usual. All the way home, he kept the secret. Once at home, he enjoyed a long shower. Then Pierrette served the traditional meal she had prepared in anticipation of his return. All through the meal, he talked about his trip, waiting for just the right moment. Once they were through eating, he could contain himself no longer. So, Koudjo finally told her the exciting news.

Pierrette sprang to her feet, raised her hands and began to praise God. She continued to praise until she was weeping. Through her tears of joy she prayed, "Oh my God, Oh my God, what Grace! Oh my God, what a wonderful God you are! That you would allow me, Pierrette, to set my feet in Your hometown? I don't deserve it, Lord. In my prayers I always refer to the New Jerusalem as the place where I will finally meet our dear Pastor Laurier and his wife Raymonde. Isn't that right my husband? Hasn't that always been my prayer?"

"Yes, Pierrette!" Koudjo agreed enthusiastically. He knew of the prayer she had prayed for years for this pastor and his wife who had supported them in their ministry. After leaving a church they had been affiliated with and launching out on their own, they had struggled. The Canadian pastor and his wife had committed to supporting them as they continued to serve the Lord.

Many times Koudjo had heard her pray: "My dear Father, I thank You for the lives of Pastor Laurier, his wife

Raymonde, and the entire Church in St-Just, Canada. I know for sure one day I will see them in the New Jerusalem where we will praise You forever. I pray that You will bless them abundantly in the name of Jesus. Amen!"

Now, she wouldn't have to wait until Jesus came back to reign in the New Jerusalem. She was being given the opportunity to visit the place where Jesus had walked, taught, and ministered while he was still on the Earth. Her delight in his news blessed his heart and all Koudjo could do was smile and rejoice with her.

....

....

Pierrette had sensed that something was on Koudjo's mind when he first got home, something that he was not ready yet to share. He had been behaving differently, almost playfully, with an air of mystery when he smiled. She had learned long ago to wait quietly until he had a chance to unwind after a long trip. So, she had waited, not dreaming that he had such wonderful news. Never in her wildest imaginings had she thought about taking such a trip with him. He was the one who travelled; she was the one who tended things at home.

In the next weeks, as they applied for visas, arranged for the care of the children, and made other preparations for the trip, Pierrette felt anticipation like that of a child at Christmas time. This trip now became Pierrette's prayer focus. After giving thanks exuberantly for such a blessing, she would pray for God's favor for the generous man who had shared his wealth to make it all possible. She prayed about every detail of their trip and for the safety of the children in their absence.

Koudjo's heart was blessed as he watched her delight in every aspect of the coming trip. For him, just being able to share such an experience with his beloved wife was a gift from God that went beyond anything he could have asked for.

……………………………………………………………………………………………

……………………………………………………………………………………………

February 18, 2016, Koudjo and Pierrette drove to Ghana to catch a 9:35 PM flight. The following day, as they were finding their way in the Istanbul airport before boarding the flight to Tel Aviv, Koudjo heard a familiar voice calling his name loudly. He turned to see two of the leaders from Nepal, Shiva and Krishna, with their wives. As introductions were made, they proceeded to the gate where their plane was waiting, excitedly chattering and laughing together. The adventure had begun.

When they landed in Tel Aviv, their excitement mounted. Though they were very tired, Koudjo felt an indescribable joy. They had made it to the Holy Land. Soon, they would be walking some of the same paths that Jesus had walked. With their own eyes, they would see many of the sights that Jesus had seen.

Pierrette's questions came back to him at that moment, "Who am I Lord?" and "I don't deserve it." He shared her sentiment at that moment. Then the answer rang clearly in his spirit:

"You are the one that I loved so much that I made provision through my Son Jesus for you to be with me for all eternity. I have placed eternity in your heart. I delight in you just as you delight in Me."

With tears stinging his eyes, he took Pierrette's hand and they prepared to set foot in the "hometown" of their Lord Jesus.

Chapter 16

After getting settled in, one of the first things they did was to take a bus trip to Caesarea Philippi. Koudjo was touched when the tour guide told them that what had been a 30 to 45 minute bus ride for them had taken Jesus more than five hours by foot. Even more notable is that hundreds of people followed him for that distance. The guide also told them that it was here that Jesus told Peter that He would build His church and the gates of hell would not prevail against it. He went on to explain the meaning of "the gates of hell" that Jesus was talking about. At that moment, Koudjo came to an understanding that Jesus was talking about launching a movement so powerful and dynamic that nothing could stop it. No religion, no amount of idolatry, rituals or any other form of paganism would be powerful enough to stop what Jesus came to do and what he had set into motion. Koudjo had always believed that Jesus spoke in terms of God's Kingdom, but now he was even more certain of this.

Later, they went out on the Sea of Galilee on a boat. As the guides told about Jesus walking on the water, Koudjo was saddened to think that these same crew members who told stories about Jesus didn't believe He was the Messiah. That same Jesus who was born here, performed miracles that they freely related, miracles that no one else had performed, was only a man to them and a way for them to make a living. There had never been such a dynamic teacher before he came, nor after He came, not to this day. Such a paradox was mind blowing to Koudjo.

Again, on the day they were to leave for home, Koudjo was amazed at the blindness of some of the people who lived in this land where Jesus had lived and taught. As he and Pierrette took one last tour of the shops before leaving, Koudjo saw a French book about prophets and prophecies that he decided to purchase. While he was paying, the owner of the shop asked about the nationalities of those in Koudjo's group. Koudjo told him that some were Nepalese, some Americans and that he and Pierrette were Togolese from West Africa. He asked for Koudjo's impressions of their trip to Israel.

"I'm excited that I was able to visit the Holy Land," Koudjo responded.

"Oh, don't be fooled about the expression 'Holy Land'," the shop keeper replied, "We have problems just like everyone else in this world. What is important is the Bible. The key to all things is to obey what the Bible says."

Koudjo left the shop thinking that, yes, what the owner of the shop said is true. The whole point of the trip would have been lost if he didn't believe that. Still, he felt uneasy about what the man said. If he was only referring to the Old Testament, the man was getting only the shadow of the truth and not the reality of the Truth. Without the personal knowledge of Jesus, the Messiah referred to in the Old Testament, the whole issue of obedience was like a smoke screen. He left praying for the smoke to be cleared for this man and for others in this very special place.

For Pierrette, being able to see the scrolls containing the Holy Scriptures that were hidden for many years was a rich experience. Because they were not destroyed, the veracity of the Bible was proven. Koudjo had heard Pierrette say many times that the best way to love future generations is to keep treasures safe for them so that when we are gone they can discover them and be blessed. She had many old things in their home to pass on when she was gone. But she also lived this out in a spiritual sense through her prayers for her children, which she knew would go on forever, long after she departed. The truths she tried to teach them along the way and these prayers would help them discover many treasures throughout their lives.

Visiting the Garden of Gethsemane created such compassion and caused a deep sense of the Lord's suffering for Pierrette. She was stricken by how very much alone Jesus was in that garden. His friends all abandoned Him. In His flesh, He felt a need for those friends. As He prayed alone, according to Luke 22:44 "And being in agony, He prayed more earnestly. Then His sweat became like drops of blood falling down to the ground."

"Koudjo," she shared later, "I think that in this life, every Christian will reach a place of loneliness where the only One for them is God. It doesn't mean we will be just one, but we'll be one with the Big One."

The time came for the TTI team and their wives to prepare say good-bye to each other and to Israel for the time being. Their lives had been enriched and their relationships were nourished in these days they had shared together in the Holy Land. They were going back to busy and often difficult lives, but it had been a time of refreshing and blessing.

As they settled into their seats for the flight home, Koudjo and Pierrette each slipped into their own place of reverie as they reflected on this wonderful trip the Lord had allowed them take. In preparation for re-entry into their busy lives, they began to think about how to incorporate what they had gained as they walked out the calling on their lives.

Chapter 17

After returning home, Koudjo was asked how the trip had changed him. As he pondered that question, many things became clear to him. Most importantly, his conviction of the veracity of the Bible increased. He was reminded of the words of Job in Job 42:5:

"I have heard of you by the hearing of the ear; But now my eye sees you."

He knew that many people from West Africa turn a trip to Israel into one of two things. First, for some it becomes such a mystical journey that everything they bring back becomes like a magic tool for healing, prosperity, power, etc. For others, it creates a business as those things are sold for their mystical powers to help finance the next trip to purchase even more things to sell. Water from the Jordan, Dead Sea water and salt, sand from the Holy Land, olive oil, bottles of wine from the wedding place, all are sold for a lot of money. Those selling these things wear a yarmulke, a skull cap worn by Orthodox Jewish men, to appear authentic. They want to impress people with the idea that they were chosen by God to do what they are doing.

For Koudjo, it was very different. When he came back, he made it a point to address this kind of deception on the radio program in Benin and on the television program in Togo. He stated strongly that only Jesus can heal and bring true prosperity. Our relationship with Him, our obedience to His principles and teachings are the real keys to healing and prosperity. He made it his mission to shed light at every opportunity in this area. Whatever he and Pierrette brought back was given freely, both materially and spiritually.

Pierrette came back from Israel with more boldness and conviction concerning her Lord Jesus. Everything that she saw and experienced adds a whole new dimension as she shares the Gospel. She came back with a new humility. Her love for others, especially perishing souls, has increased. Her service for the brethren has also increased.

"I saw with my own eyes the places where my Lord Jesus humbled Himself and suffered for me. If my Lord Jesus could walk for hours, could serve others as He did, and suffer loneliness and rejection, no sacrifice I have to make is too much in furthering His Kingdom."

Koudjo loved hearing Pierrette's thoughts and reminiscing with her about their trip. On one evening after they had had a good time of conversation, Koudjo suggested that they make a list of those they were thankful for and pray blessings for those people. They began the process that night. And Koudjo began to pray.

"Lord Jesus, first of all and above all, Pierrette and I thank You for Your Gift of Salvation! We thank You for choosing us to be members of Your Body. You are the One who took the way of the cross and chose us to follow You into Your Kingdom work. We thank You for Dr. David Nelms, Founder of TTI. We thank You for Jared Nelms, Dr. David's son, and one of my best friends. We give special thanks for Pastors Jimmy Carroll and Chris Stevens for making our trip to Israel possible. We thank You for our

Canadian Partners of La Bible Parle, Pastors Jeff Laurrin, Real Gaudreault, Richard Cote, Claude Hurteau, Laurier Mercier, and special thanks to Paul and Martin Tremblay. Bless them richly, Lord."

Then, Koudjo remembered years ago what Pastor Jeff had told him when he was in Africa.

"Koudjo, you need to write a book about your ministry. I am ready to publish it."

That had been a long time ago, but Koudjo knew that God's timing is the best. He added one more name to the list.

"Lord, we thank you for Brenda Ring who is finally writing my story. We ask You to bless her."

Koudjo knew that there were many others who would be added to the list at another time. There were many who had blessed their lives and who had walked with them and would continue to in the future. They had all been called into the Body of Christ and were working together for the furtherance of His Kingdom. One day, they would all be together in the New Jerusalem. The Holy Spirit reminded him of a scripture when his prayer had ended. As he shared it with Pierrette, they felt the presence of the Lord as strongly as they had when they walked the streets that He had walked.

"But as it is written, Eye hath not seen, nor ear heard, neither have entered into the heart of man, the things which God hath prepared for them that love Him." (I Corinthians 2:9)

Made in the USA
Columbia, SC
25 November 2023